SPECTRUM WRITING
by Iris Schwartz

CONTENTS

1997 © McGraw-Hill Learning Materials

Project Editor: Sandra Kelley
Text: Design and Production by Harry Chester Associates
Illustrated by Connie Maltese

Things To Remember About Writing

WRITING

- Be sure that every story you write has a main idea.
- Tell how to do something in order.
- Use order words like <u>first</u> and <u>next</u>.
- Use <u>er</u> and <u>est</u> to compare things.
- Use your senses when you describe something.
- If you write about a problem, think of the best answer to the problem.
- Choose clear words when you write.
- Use capital letters for names and sentence beginnings.
- End telling sentences and questions with the right marks.
- Proofread what you write to make it better.

unit 1
Writing Main Ideas

The **main idea** tells what something is all about.

 Be sure that every story you write has a main idea.

Choose a title that tells the main idea.

Choose clear naming words when you write.

Finding the right group

A. Look at each picture. Draw a line under the group you see. Then finish the sentence.

| animals |
| trees |
| <u>flowers</u> |

This is a group of _flowers_ .

| cars |
| fruits |
| dogs |

This is a group of _____ .

| letters |
| birds |
| books |

This is a group of _____ .

B. Look at each group. Cross out what does not belong. Then write a sentence about the group.

hats

This is a group of hats.

shoes

balls

numbers

C. Look at each group. Draw something else that belongs in the group.

This is a group of things to wear.

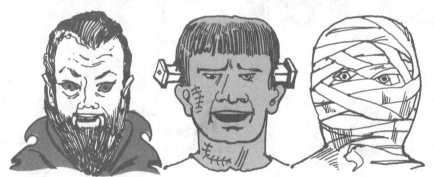

This is a group of monsters.

D. Read each group of words. Then write the group name on the line.

Family	Colors	Animals
_____	_____	_____
red	father	fish
blue	mother	goat
yellow	children	cat

 Write a group name on a piece of paper. Draw three pictures that belong in the group. Then write the word for each picture.

Writing the main idea of a picture

The **main idea** of a picture tells what the picture is all about.

A. Find the main idea for each picture.
Then draw a line under it.

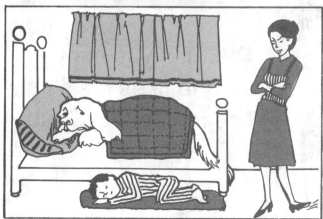

Her feet are wet.
Her head is wet.
<u>Her hands are wet.</u>

The bird looks funny.
The man is kind.
The children work.

Mother is happy.
A boy gives up his bed.
A boy plays ball.

A. Draw a line under the main idea.

A boy reads at night.
A boy is at school.
A boy is sleeping.

Yoko likes to eat.
Yoko does nothing.
Yoko likes to build.

The family is happy.
No one likes his singing.
The family feels cold.

B. Look at each picture. Then write the
main idea.

_____

- - - - - - - - - - - - - - - - - - -

_____

- - - - - - - - - - - - - - - - - - -

_____

_____

- - - - - - - - - - - - - - - - - - -

_____

- - - - - - - - - - - - - - - - - - -

_____

 Draw a picture on a piece of paper.
Write the main idea on your paper.

Writing the main idea of a story

lesson 3

The main idea of a story tells what the story is all about.

A. Find the main idea for each story. Then draw a line under it.

Billy is a dog walker. He walks dogs before school. He walks dogs after school. When Billy finishes, he has fun. He takes his own dog for a walk.

The main idea is

Billy goes to school.

Billy walks many dogs.

First, Pam puts on her dress. Next, she puts on her hat. Last, she gets into bed. Pam wants to be ready for school tomorrow!

The main idea is

Pam finds a kitten.

Pam gets ready for school early.

A. Draw a line under the main idea.

Father takes the airplane. He shows Jenny how to play with it. He shows her over and over again. The plane is for Jenny. But Father has all the fun.

The main idea is
    Father plays with an airplane.
    Father goes to work.
    Father gets a car.

Jack wants to get a letter. He asks for one day after day. At last, Mrs. Hill brings Jack a letter. Jack gets the letter A.

The main idea is
    Mrs. Hill works hard.
    Jack plays ball.
    Jack gets a letter.

B. Read each story. Write the main idea.

Tom made a little man. He gave the man many things to do. But the little man just loved to work. Now he does not want to stop.

_____

- - - - - - - - - - - - - - - - - -

_____

- - - - - - - - - - - - - - - - - -

_____

Bee wants to try new food. First, it tries rabbit food. Next, it tries dog food. Last, it tries food for children. Now Bee does not want any more new food. It is happy to eat bee food.

_____

- - - - - - - - - - - - - - - - - -

_____

- - - - - - - - - - - - - - - - - -

_____

Write a story about something you do in school. Use another piece of paper. Write the main idea under your story.

Writing a title

A **title** is a name for a picture or a story.

A. Look at the picture. Draw a line under the best title.

A good title is

    A Man Drives a Car

    A Man Reads a Story

    A Man Cooks Food

A. Draw a line under the best title.

A good title is

    The Story Is Funny

    The Story Puts Children to Sleep

    The Children Are Working

B. Read the next story. Find the best title. Write it on the line over the story.

_____

- -

_____

My big bag has everything I need. It has food when I want to eat. It has a story when I want to read. It even has my kitten when I want to play.

A good title is

    My Big Bag

    My Big House

    The Big Party

C. Read this story. Think of a title. Write it on the line.

_____
- -
_____

    Pete has a new rain hat. He takes it off when it rains. He puts it on when it stops. Pete does not want his new rain hat to get wet!

D. Choose one of the titles below. Draw a line under it. Then write a story that goes with the title.

    If Children Ran the School
    A Funny Pet
    If Snow Was Green

_____
- -
_____

_____
- -
_____

_____
- -
_____

_____
- -
_____

Write On Pick another title from **D.** Or think of your own. Then write a story that fits your title.

Choosing naming words

person

thing

king

elephant

The **person** walks the **thing**.   The **king** walks the **elephant**.

The naming words in the second sentence are clear. They give a better picture of what is happening.

A. Read the sentence. Think of clearer naming words. Write them on the lines. Then draw a picture to go with your new sentence.

The **animal** wears the **thing**.

The _____ wears the _____.

B. Each box has clear naming words.
Write three sentences. Use two
naming words in each sentence.

teacher

monster

kangaroo

cowboy

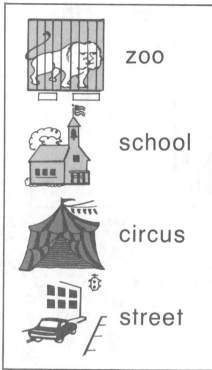

zoo

school

circus

street

horn

hot dog

telephone

TV

The kangaroo is on TV.

Write person, place, and thing on
three pieces of paper. Write three
clear naming words for each word.
Then use your names in sentences.

Post-Test

1. Read each group below. Cross out the word that does not belong in each group.

hat	tree	sun
cat	truck	star
dog	flower	four
bird	bush	moon

2. Look at the picture. Then write a sentence that tells the main idea.

_____

- -

_____

3. Read the story. Then write a title for it.

_____

- -

_____

Dana found a pretty rug in the woods. She sat down on it to rest. Suddenly the rug began to move. Soon Dana was flying over the trees on her magic rug!

unit 2
Writing in Sequence

Sequence means order.

 Use order words like <u>first</u> and <u>next</u>.

Tell how to do something in order.

Write story parts in order.

Use capital letters for names and sentence beginnings.

Writing picture stories

A. Look at the pictures below. They can
tell a story. Put them in order. Write
<u>First</u>, <u>Next</u>, and <u>Last</u> under the pictures.

First   Last   Next

A. Write First, Next, and Last under the pictures.

_____   _____   _____

_ _ _ _ _ _ _ _   _ _ _ _ _ _ _ _   _ _ _ _ _ _ _ _

_____   _____   _____

B. Finish each story. Draw the last picture.

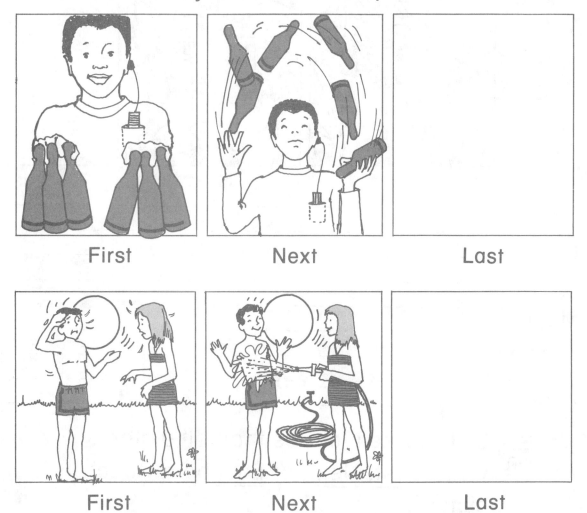

First   Next   Last

First   Next   Last

B. Draw the last picture.

First   Next   Last

C. Finish the story. Draw the last picture.
Then write a sentence about each picture.

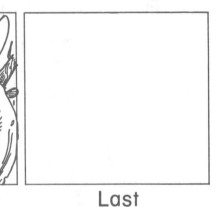

First   Next   Last

_____

First, _____

_____

Next, _____

_____

Last, _____

 Draw three pictures that tell a story.
Write <u>First</u>, <u>Next</u>, or <u>Last</u> below each
picture.

2 Using order words

First

Next

Last

First, I take a peanut.

Next, I try to catch it.

Last, I clean up.

Words like First, Next, and Last help
tell a story in **order.**

A. Put the sentences below in order. Write
First, Next, or Last in front of each one.

First

Next

Last

_____, Juan went to the Lost and Found.

_____, Juan found his pet elephant.

_____, he told what he lost.

A. Write <u>First</u>, <u>Next</u>, or <u>Last</u> in front of each sentence.

First Next Last

_____
_____, they took a walk.

_____
_____, Fay and her dog ate breakfast.

_____
_____, they got ready.

First Next Last

_____
_____, Al bought a big apple.

_____
_____, Al went to the Big Food Store.

_____
_____, he saw lots of big food.

B. Write a sentence about each picture.
Use an order word in each sentence.

First   Then   Last

First, Mo jumped over the bar.

Draw three pictures that tell a story.
Write <u>First</u>, <u>Next</u>, or <u>Last</u> under each
one. Then write three sentences
about the pictures. Use order words.

Telling how to do something

Here is how to make a fan.

First

Next

Finally

First, take a piece of paper.

Next, fold the paper.

Finally, you have a fan.

A. The pictures below show how to teach a dog to sit. Write sentences that tell how to do it. Order your sentences.

First

Then

Last

First, _____

_____

Then, _____

_____

Last, _____

B. The pictures below show how to make a walkie-talkie. Write sentences that tell how to do it. Order your sentences.

First

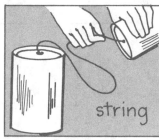
Second

Third

First, _____

_____

Second, _____

_____

Third, _____

C. The pictures below show how to make breakfast. Write sentences that tell how to do it. Order your sentences.

First

Then

Finally

First, _____

_____

Then, _____

_____

Finally, _____

D. The pictures below show how to play tag. Write sentences that tell how to do it. Be sure your sentences are in order.

First   Next   Last

_____

First, _____

_____

Next, _____

_____

Last, _____

 Draw three pictures that show how to do something. Write <u>First</u>, <u>Second</u>, and <u>Third</u> below the pictures. Then use the order words in sentences. Tell about each picture.

Writing story parts in order

All stories have a **beginning**, a **middle**, and an **end.**

A. The pictures below can tell a story. Put them in order. Write <u>beginning</u>, <u>middle</u>, or <u>end</u> below each picture.

_____

_____

Beginning

_____

_____

_____

B. Each group of pictures tells a story.
Write a sentence that tells about each
part of the story.

Beginning   Middle   End

Beginning: The girl bought a fish.

Middle: _____

End: _____

Beginning   Middle   End

Beginning: _____

Middle: _____

End: _____

C. Put these stories in order. Write
Beginning, Middle, and End on the
lines.

_____ : Now Robin just wants
to sit in the sun.

_____ : But the water got her
feet cold.

_____ : First, Robin ran to
the water.

_____ : Sally wants to
sleep.

_____ : So she puts Birdy in
another room.

_____ : But Birdy is talking
loudly.

_____ : Now his pocket is
very wet.

_____ : Jim had a snowball
in his hand.

_____ : Then he put it in his
pocket.

 Draw three pictures that tell a story.
Write Beginning, Middle, and End
below the pictures. Then write your
story in order.

5 Using capital letters

The first word of a sentence begins
with a **capital letter**.

 This is a sentence.

A. Write three sentences about the picture.
 Begin each sentence with a capital letter.

Happy
Birthday

The big box is by the door.

Names begin with capital letters.

<u>A</u>my   <u>R</u>ex   <u>L</u>uis

B. Name everyone in this picture. Then write three sentences telling about the picture. Use a name in each sentence.

_____

- -

_____

- -

_____

- -

_____

 Write a sentence that tells about a friend. Use capital letters where they belong.

Post-Test

1. Put the pictures in order. Write <u>First</u>, <u>Next</u>, and <u>Last</u> below the pictures.

_____   _____   _____

_____   _____   _____

2. Tell how you play on a slide in a playground. Write two sentences.

_____

First, _____

_____

Then, _____

3. The story below is out of order. Put the sentences in order. Write <u>Beginning</u>, <u>Middle</u>, and <u>End</u>.

_____

_____ : Meg's dog Whitey looked gray.

_____ : Now Whitey looks like his name again.

_____ : Meg washed Whitey in the tub.

32

unit **3**
Writing Comparisons

When you **compare** things, you tell how they are the same or different.

 Use <u>er</u> and <u>than</u> to compare two things.

Use <u>er</u> and <u>est</u> to compare three things.

Use <u>like</u> or <u>as</u> to compare different things.

Use describing words to make your sentences clear.

Comparing two pictures

When you **compare** things, you tell how they are the same or different.

A. Look at each picture. Then finish each sentence. Use the words in the box to compare the two things.

| taller than |
| shorter than |

Ted is ___taller than___ Len.

Len is ___shorter than___ Ted.

| bigger than |
| smaller than |

Tub is _____ Biff.

Biff is _____ Tub.

B. Compare the things in each picture.
Use the words in the box. Write whole
sentences.

| longer than |
| shorter than |

Bo is longer than Dee.

Dee is shorter than Bo.

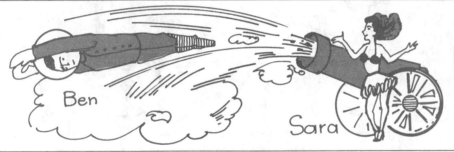

| faster than |
| slower than |

| higher than |
| lower than |

C. Look at the picture. Think of ways to compare the people and the animals. Then write three sentences. Use the words in the boxes to help you.

| bigger than
smaller than | longer than
shorter than | taller than
shorter than |

_____

- - - - - - - - - - - - - - - - - - - -

_____

- - - - - - - - - - - - - - - - - - - -

_____

- - - - - - - - - - - - - - - - - - - -

_____

Write On Draw two animals you see at the zoo. Then write a sentence to compare the animals. Use a word from a box above in your sentence.

2

Comparing three pictures

You can use one word to compare three things.

A. Compare the things below. Read the words in the box. Then finish each sentence.

big	bigger	biggest

Cod is _big_ .

Fin is _bigger_ .

Mac is _biggest_ .

wet	wetter	wettest

Lynn is _____ .

Dan is _____ .

Sue is _____ .

B. Use the words in the box to compare the three things. Write whole sentences.

funny
funnier
funniest

fat
fatter
fattest

B. Write sentences to compare the three things.

| small |
| smaller |
| smallest |

| happy |
| happier |
| happiest |

 Draw three people. Write their names.
Then write <u>big</u>, <u>bigger</u>, and <u>biggest</u>
below the pictures to compare them.

Comparing people

You can compare how people look.

A. Compare the people in the picture.
Use one set of words from each box.

Gran is _____ Jan.

younger than
older than

Gran is _____ Jan.

taller than
shorter than

Gran's hair is _____ Jan's.

lighter than
darker than

You can compare how people feel.

B. Use the words in the box to compare the boys.

| happier than |
| sadder than |

Frank is _____ Greg.

Greg is _____ Frank.

You can also compare what people say.

C. Read the sentences below. Write who is speaking on each line.

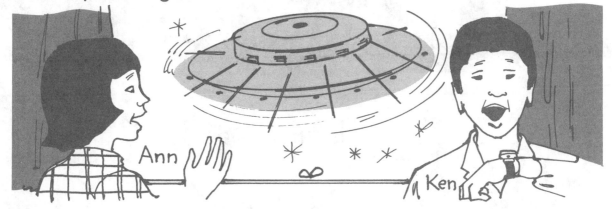

Ken: I must get some sleep for school tomorrow.

Ann: I want to see the moon people better.

C. Tell who is speaking.

Kay

Nan

_____

\- - - - - - - - - - -
_____ : That hat looks silly.

_____

\- - - - - - - - - -
_____ : My friends will like this hat.

Fred

Paco

_____

\- - - - - - - - - - -
_____ : It is fun to sleep out.

_____

\- - - - - - - - - -
_____ : I want my bed at home.

 Draw two friends playing. Write their names. Then write two sentences. Tell what each friend is saying.

Comparing with like and as

The children are <u>as</u> silly <u>as</u> monkeys.
The children are <u>like</u> monkeys.

You can tell about one thing by comparing it to something else. You use <u>like</u> or <u>as</u> to compare.

A. Look at each picture. Circle the best words to finish the sentences. Write the words on both lines.

(an airplane)
a house

I go as fast as **an airplane**.

I go like **an airplane**.

A. Circle the best word. Write it on both lines.

ball
train

_____

His tail is as long as a _____ .

His tail is like a _____ .

ant
elephant

_____

This rock is as big as an _____ .

This rock is like an _____ .

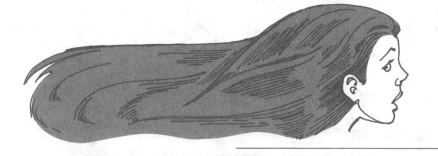

grass
fire

_____

Her hair is as red as _____ .

Her hair is like _____ .

B. Here is part of a letter Beth wrote. Finish her sentences. Tell about the rabbit by comparing it to other things.

Dear James,

   Here is a picture of my new rabbit. I named him James after you.

bee
kangaroo
cloud
bean

↖James bug
mouse
snowball
horse

James is as white as a _____.

He is as little as a _____.

He can sit as still as a _____.

But then he jumps like a _____.

And I race like a _____ to catch him.

Compare a person to an animal. Draw a picture of the person next to the animal. Tell how they are the same.

Using describing words

How can you help the boy? You can say:
   Please bring my <u>red</u> coat.

<u>Red</u> is a describing word.

A. Look at each picture. Then choose the best describing word. Put it in the sentence.

big
small

I have a _____ spot on my dress.

A. Choose two describing words for
each sentence.

warm
sunny

cold
wet

_____ _____

It was a _____, _____ day.

kind
old

mean
young

_____ _____

She is a _____, _____ woman.

B. Use one describing word from **A** to
finish each sentence below.

_____

1. The _____ man lives on the moon.

_____

2. My hat is _____.

 Draw a picture of someone you know.
Write a sentence about the person.
Use one or two describing words in
your sentence.

Post-Test

1. Use the words in the box to compare an apple and a grape.

| smaller than |
| larger than |

An apple is _____ a grape.

A grape is _____ an apple.

2. Use the words in the box to compare the pictures. Write whole sentences.

| fast |
| faster |
| fastest |

_____

_____

_____

_____

3. Finish each sentence about Peg's treehouse.

The treehouse is as big as _____.

The ladder is as long as _____.

The treehouse looks like _____.

48

unit **4**
Writing Details

Details are small parts that make a whole.

 Use your senses when you describe something.

Use describing words to tell how a person looks and feels.

When you write an invitation, tell when and where.

End telling sentences and questions with the right marks.

Writing with your senses

You use your **senses** to

see

taste

hear

smell

touch

A. Look at the things in the pictures.
Read the sense words under them.
Then circle the ways you can learn
about each thing.

skunk

(see)   hear   (smell)   taste   (touch)

drums

see   hear   smell   taste   touch

peanut

see   hear   smell   taste   touch

B. Look at the pictures. Circle the ways you can learn about each thing. Then write a sentence for each. Use a sense word in your sentence.

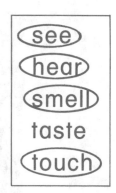

see
hear
smell
taste
touch

I see a yellow fire.

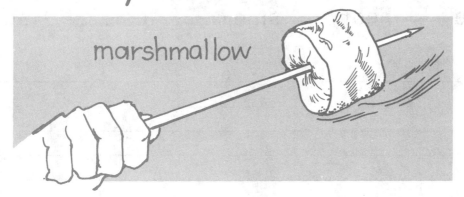

see
hear
smell
taste
touch

see
hear
smell
taste
touch

C. Here is a picture of Jerry camping.
Make believe you are Jerry. Write
three sentences about the picture.
Use a sense word in each sentence.

owl
water
fire
raccoon
bugs

see   hear   smell   taste   touch

Dear Mom,

_____

- -

_____

_____

- -

_____

_____

- -

_____

_____

- -

_____

Love,
Jerry

 Draw a picture of something at home.
Then write the senses you can use to
learn about it.

2 Writing about a person

You can tell how a person looks.

A. Tell about hair. Use the words in the box. Finish the sentences.

| short | long | curly | straight |

Andy has _____ hair.

Meg has _____ hair.

Rosa has _____ hair.

Jill has _____ hair.

B. Tell about what people wear. Use the
words in the box. Finish the sentences.

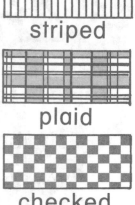

striped

plaid

checked

Mel has a _____ shirt.

Mel has _____ pants.

Carol has a _____ dress.

C. Tell what Pedro will wear. Write two
whole sentences.

suit

tie

_____

_____

_____

_____

You can tell how a person feels.

D. Look at the people in the picture. Use the words in the box to tell how they feel.

happy   sad   mad   surprised   scared

Ruth feels _____.

Nick feels _____.

Dora feels _____.

 Tell about yourself on a piece of paper. Tell how you look. Tell what you like to wear. Tell how you feel.

Lesson 3

Writing riddles

Let's all play The Riddle Game!

A. The TV man will tell about something.
Write what it is on the line.

It is long.
It has no feet.

_____

It is _____.

a kangaroo

It can make a picture.
It comes in many colors.

_____

It is _____.

a snake

It hops around.
It keeps its baby in a pocket.

_____

It is _____.

a crayon

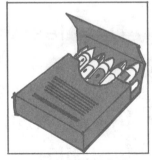

B. Now write your own riddles. Write two sentences to tell about each thing below. Use the words in the box to help you.

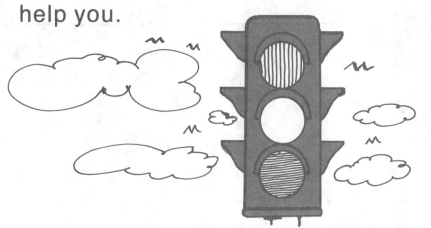

red
green
cars
stop
go

_____

- -

_____

- -

_____

It is a traffic light.

up
down
building
open
close

_____

- -

_____

- -

_____

It is an elevator.

Now the Riddle Game comes into your home!

C. Draw something you can find in your home. Then write three sentences to tell about your picture.

It is a _____.

Write On Draw a picture of something outside. Then write three sentences about it. Read your riddle to the class. See if anyone can guess your picture.

Writing an invitation

An **invitation** is a letter. It can ask someone to come to a party. An invitation tells—

1. the kind of party
2. the day and time of the party
3. where the party will be

A. Invite a friend to a Valentine's Day Party at your home. Valentine's Day is February 14.

_____
_____
Dear _____,
_____
_____
I am giving a _____
_____
_____
party. It is on February _____.
_____
_____
It starts at _____ o'clock. My home is at
_____
_____.

B. Invite someone to a Halloween Party at your school. Look at the days in October to find the date.

Dear _____,

We are giving a _____.

It is on _____, October _____.

It starts at _____ o'clock. It is in Room _____

of _____ School.

Do-o-o-o come!

October

Sunday	Monday	Tuesday	Wednesday	Thursday	Friday	Saturday
			1	2	3	4
5	6	7	8	9	10	11
12	13	14	15	16	17	18
19	20	21	22	23	24	25
26	27	28	29	30	(31)	

C. Invite someone to a swim party. Choose when and where to have your party.

Dear _____,

    I am giving a _____.

It is on _____, July _____.

It starts at _____ o'clock. It is

at _____.

July

Sunday	Monday	Tuesday	Wednesday	Thursday	Friday	Saturday
			1	2	3	4
5	6	7	8	9	10	11
12	13	14	15	16	17	18
19	20	21	22	23	24	25
26	27	28	29	30	31	

Write an invitation to your birthday party. Tell when your birthday is. Tell where your party will be. Use the invitations in this lesson to help you.

Writing telling sentences and questions

A **telling sentence** tells something. It begins with a capital letter. It ends with a ☐.

A. Look at the picture below. Write a story about it. Tell three things you see.

Elephant on Main Street

An elephant is in the street.

A **question** asks something. It begins
with a capital letter. It ends with a ?

B. You ask questions to find out things.
Ask these people about their jobs.
Write three questions. Use the words
in the box to start them.

How
Where
What
Why
When
Can

Fireman   Doctor   Policeman

How do you put out fires?

 Write two questions to ask in class.
Then read your questions. Let some
children answer them.

Post-Test

1. Circle the senses you can use to learn about a drum.

    see   hear   smell   taste   touch

2. Make up a riddle about an umbrella. Write two sentences that tell about the umbrella.

_____

_____

_____

_____

It is an umbrella.

3. Write a telling sentence about a person on TV.

_____

Write a question you could ask this person.

_____

unit 5
Writing About Cause and Effect

A **cause** tells what makes something happen. An **effect** is what happens.

  One way to write a story is to think of a problem. Then write an answer to the problem.

When you write a letter of complaint, tell what is wrong.

Proofread what you write to make it better.

Cause and effect pictures

Cause

Effect

Cause: Lee hugs his pet porcupine.

Effect: Lee gets cuts from his pet.

A. Look at the pictures below. Draw a
line to match the cause with the effect.

Cause   Effect

A. Draw a line to match the cause with the effect.

Cause | Effect

B. The picture below shows a cause. Draw a picture to show the effect.

Cause | Effect

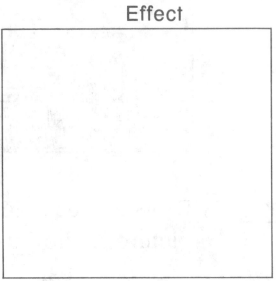

B. Draw pictures to show the effects.

Cause   Effect

 Draw a cause picture and an effect picture. Write <u>Cause</u> and <u>Effect</u> under your pictures.

Writing cause and effect sentences

Cause: I am on my head.
Effect: All my friends look funny.

A. Look at the picture below. Read the cause sentence. Then write a sentence that tells the effect.

Cause: Willa's hands get cold at work.

_____

- -

Effect:_____

A. Write sentences that tell each effect.

Cause: Annie gets pennies day after day.

Effect: _____

Cause: Hal had many friends at his party.

Effect: _____

Cause: It was too small for Bobby.

Effect: _____

B. Look at each picture below. Read the sentence that tells the effect. Write a sentence that tells the cause.

Cause:_____

Effect: So we saw it again and again.

Cause:_____

Effect: So I did not put in any water.

 Take two pieces of paper. Draw a cause picture on one. Draw an effect picture on the other. Let the class guess which is the cause and which is the effect.

3 Writing story problems

Problem: The boy thinks that a very
big animal is near.

A. The picture below shows a problem.
Write the problem below the picture.

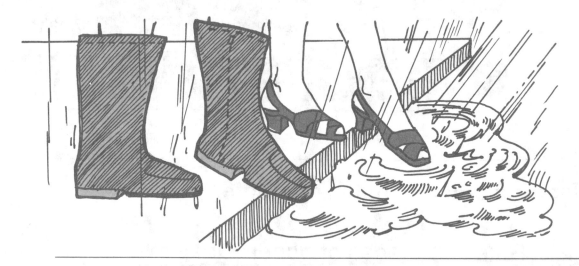

Problem:_____

_____

A. Write the problem you see.

Problem: _____

Problem: _____

B. Write the problem you see in the picture. Then write an answer to the problem.

Problem: He carries too much.

Answer: He should use the wagon.

Problem: _____

_____

Answer: _____

 Draw a picture that shows a problem.
Write the problem under the picture.
Then write an answer to the problem.

Writing a letter of complaint

Complaint: This coat is too big.

Telling what you think is wrong is called a **complaint.**

A. The person in the picture has a complaint. Write what the complaint is.

Complaint:_____

_____

_____

A. Write a complaint for each picture.

Complaint:_____

Complaint:_____

Complaint:_____

B. Your new dog Rags is acting up. Write a letter of complaint to the pet store. Tell what is wrong with Rags. Use the picture to help you.

Dear Pet Store Owner:

_____

- -

_____

- -

_____

_____

- -

_____

_____

- -

_____

_____

- -

_____

 Draw a picture of something that you do not like. Then write a sentence that tells your complaint.

Proofreading

Proofreading means reading over something to make it better.

A. The story below does not have capital letters. The sentences do not end with a ⬚. or a ?⬚ Read over the story. Put in what is missing.

Ⓞne day Ⓑetty got very big now her

house is too little for her what will

betty do will she buy a bigger house

No. she will wake up from her dream

B. The story below does not have clear naming words. It has no describing words. Make the story better. Add words and sentences. Use the picture to help you.

He walks down the street. People see things. They do not see him.

Mr. Day walks down the busy street.

 Write a story about something that can never happen. Then read over your story to make it better.

Post-Test

1. Write a cause and effect sentence.

_____

Cause:_____

_____

Effect:_____

2. Write the problem and an answer.

_____

_____

_____

3. You are Val. Write your complaint.

_____

Complaint:_____

Post-Test Answers; pg 16

1. hat   truck   four
2. Wording will vary, but the sentences should convey the idea that the cats want some of the boy's fish.
3. Answers will vary, but should include the idea of a magic rug or Dana's magic rug.

Post-Test Answers; pg 32

1. Next   First   Last
2. First, I climb (or go) up the slide.
   Then, I slide down.
3. Beginning
   End
   Middle

Post-Test Answers; pg 48

1. larger than
   smaller than
2. Wording may vary. Answers should convey the following ideas:
   Jen is fast.
   Len is faster than Jen.
   Ben is the fastest.
3. Answers will vary.

Post-Test Answers; pg 64

1. see, hear, touch
2. Answers will vary. Here is one possibility:
   It keeps you dry.
   It goes up and down.
3. Answers will vary. Be sure the first sentence ends with a period and the second with a question mark.

Post-Test Answers; pg 80

1. The wording of the answers will vary.
   Accept sentences that convey the following cause and effect.
   The boy did not look where he was going. (or)
   The boy was riding carelessly.
   The bicycle crashed.
2. People cannot see the stop sign.
   The branches should be cut away.
3. Hal's radio is too loud. (or)
   Hal should not play his radio.